Tea

Overcome Adversities

While

Discovering Life Skills

Through martial arts training

"Everything we do as teachers must ensure that the child's inherent desire to learn is kept alive."

~ Robert John Meehan

Dedication

I dedicate this work to my wife, Monique S. Dabney, for her patience and organizing all of my thoughts; my two daughters, Desirée S. Dabney and Alexis B. Dabney, for their willingness to learn from a lecturing father; and, to both my mother, Rosa L. Dabney, and mother-in-law, Gwendolyn Poles-Sands, for being parents of Faith and Hope.

Introduction

Shortly, after my kid returned home from her first year of college, a surprising thing happened...

"Mom and Dad I have something to tell you," – now after holding our breath bracing for the worst – the words that every parent who believes in tough love hopes to hear is – "I didn't understand why you were so tough on me, but now I want to say...Thanks."

And while there isn't a set recipe for raising successful children, teaching your child life skills is not only important for self-care and sufficiency— it also allows them to feel empowered.

All parents want their child/children to do well in school, stay out of trouble and go on to do amazing things as adults but, much of it comes down to *"6574 days of parenting."*

That is the number of days before your loved ones celebrate their 18th birthday.

Are you preparing your child to be dependent or independent?

"The great mistake good parents make is doing too much for their children,"

Dr. Edward Hallowell, M.D. Child Psychiatrist and Author

What must we do to be successful in parenting?

What are the basic factors that any person must face in order to survive?

Today, there are many ideas and advice about parenting that could be overwhelming for some. The *6574 Principles for Purposeful Parenting* is not an idea or advice, it's a comprehensive in-depth insight for raising happy, healthy, independent children to become successful teens and adults.

We've all heard these child rearing clichés before: "They are only little once." "It takes a village to raise a child." "Not for the faint of heart"

"You'll miss these days (with young children tugging you in every direction)." "The days are long, but the years are short."

Most of them are true statements and they all take on a whole new meaning when you have children of your own.

"Parents, Time Passes So Quickly" and you figuratively have 6,574 days, 157,776 hours and 9,466,560 minutes before your child/children turn 18 years of age. When you break it down and look at it, and think about how long those minutes sometimes feel when you are in the thick of raising these little ones, it's hard to think of this time as being 'short.'

"Efforts and courage are not enough without purpose and direction."

—John F. Kennedy

About The Author

Please keep in mind that my story is a short glance at what lessons I've personally learned along my journey. Within the book there is an in-depth look at the life lessons being taught at Competitive Edge Karate from my experiences, followed by real stories from students and parents.

When parents and teachers work as partners, children do better in school and at home. When working together as partners, it's been found that parents and teachers communicate more effectively, develop stronger relationships with one another and develop skills to support children's behaviors and learning.

My Adversities, My Path, My Process is

My Story

This is a story about a shy, introverted kid who started training in the martial arts in 1978 at the age of 14. By July 1981 at the age of 17, he had earned his First Degree Black Belt and won a Featherweight Amateur Kickboxing Championship Title.

That shy, introverted kid was I, the author, Roger W. Dabney.

The Adversities

My shyness was a mild feeling of discomfort and insecurity with new situations, which eventually I grew out of because of my martial arts training. But there's another discomfort that I've battled with and that's Dyslexia. Yes, I'm Dyslexic.

Dyslexia is a visual learning condition with the processing of words or numbers. Through some research on the matter, I discovered the good and the bad. Dyslexics tend to be exceptionally curious, creative, highly intelligent, multi-dimensional thinkers and more intuitive than average.

Their distinctive *mode of thought* also *produces* the *gift of mastery*: once they have learned something experientially, they understand it *on such a deep level* that they know how to do it *intuitively without thinking* about how.

It is estimated that between 5-10% of the population have dyslexia, but this number can also be as high as 17%.

Here is a list of some very talented and famous dyslexics: Albert Einstein, Thomas Edison, Alexander Graham Bell, Leonardo da Vinci, Erin Brokovich, Walt Disney, Winston Churchill, Cher, Whoopi Goldberg, Tommy

Hilfiger, Steven Spielberg, Richard Branson, and Steve Jobs.

"Everybody is a genius. But if you judge a fish by its ability to climb a tree, it will live its whole life believing that it is stupid."

~Albert Einstein

In July of 1981 while assisting in my first karate class at American Open Style Karate School located in Ashland, VA, my adversities were about to be exposed. I realized I had to talk in front of people and read the karate curriculum aloud to the class for each belt level. I was training under an instructor who was tough and loved to explain techniques and speak in front of the class. My Dyslexia could become challenging and hinder my ability to teach.

But because I was so motivated about the opportunity to teach, I read each belt level curriculum's sheet every day, while visualizing myself teaching class.

"Learn It – Memorize It – Master It"

Master your abilities with relentless efforts. Become the best student ever by studying longer and just working harder.

~ *Roger Dabney*

The Path

At the early age of 17, I knew what I wanted to share with the students had ***absolutely nothing to do with fighting.*** But what do you tell a class of 6 thru 9-year-old kids, who are excited about having a kickboxing champion teach their class? And, that he's not going to be teaching kickboxing techniques? I had to figure out how to explain to them that you *first* must develop the right mindset to be a champion in both martial arts and life. Looking back at it now, this scenario became another perfect test for me. I just had given up two years of my childhood fun to become the Virginia State Amateur Featherweight Kickboxing Champion and I could share that process with them, as long as I teach some kickboxing techniques.

Staying dedicated to my goals of becoming a better martial arts instructor, I focused on teaching one good class at a time. Now, I'm turning 18 years old and still extremely ambitious about kickboxing training and graduating from high school. This ambition led to a long talk with my mother, who was my biggest fan. She explained to me the importance *of believing in yourself and not listen to others. It's your dream that's important not another person's idea for you.* My martial arts instructor/fight coach/trainer, Danny W. Wilson, who I had met 4 years earlier teaching karate at the local civic center in Ashland, VA, advised me, "You're a very talented fighter and you've made some big gains in a very short period of time and with the proper training and guidance, you could be a champion." That's how and why I decided to turn professional and pursue my kickboxing career. This would mean relinquishing my amateur status to become a professional athlete and accept compensation for the sport of Full Contact Karate.

About two years into competing as a professional, I took a fight in Washington, DC on a two weeks notice and it changed my kickboxing and martial arts paths forever. I got an opportunity to work with Jeff Smith and Michael Coles, two of the top martial artists and kickboxing champions in the world. But in order to train and compete with them, I would have to move. After another long talk with my mom, I decided to pack my car, move to Northern Virginia and follow my dreams. This took my kickboxing development and boxing skills to another level of training, by allowing me to compete against a higher level of competition. There is one particular fight in Philadelphia, PA that comes to my mind. I was scheduled to fight against a fighter from the Virgin Islands. After reading over his fight record of 20-5-2 and *my* fight record at the time was 7-2-1, it was clear that the fun of being a fighter was over.

The unexpected lesson was being introduced to Tae Kwon Do training. I must say it was really cool but very intimidating at the beginning. I went from a 30 to 40-student martial arts school to an operation with 5 to 7 locations and thousands of students.

It truly would take another book to share all the martial arts lessons; teaching methods; inspirational and motivational encouragement; people; students; instructors; and, my overall experience of being there at that time. But, I'm very grateful and blessed to have had that opportunity to learn from some of best martial artists in the world. As I continue my personal and business relationships with them, let me introduce them to you.

Jeff Smith is a multi-talented Martial Arts

Master, World Kickboxing Champion, innovator, teacher, coach, mentor, Taekwondo Hall of Famer and leader. Grand Master Jeff Smith has influenced millions of martial artists around the world, both directly and indirectly. One of his title defense matches was the co-main event on the undercard for the Ali vs. Frazier "Thrilla in Manila."

Michael Coles was promoted to Head Instructor of the Jhoon Rhee Institute. Grandmaster Michael Coles traveled throughout the United States and abroad competing as a member of the Jhoon Rhee Superstars. Master Coles was the PKA United States Full Contact Welterweight Champion from 1979 to 1981. During this period, he served as sparring partner for World Champion "Sugar" Ray Leonard.

They both were martial arts and kickboxing champions, but more importantly incredible and motivated martial arts instructors. This is where I got introduced to world renowned Grandmaster Jhoon Rhee. As I personally didn't get the opportunity to work directly with GM Rhee, it was very clear from Coles and Smith that GM Rhee's influence on them was an essential part of their success.

Grandmaster Jhoon Rhee is known as "the Father of American Tae Kwon Do." Jhoon Rhee was the first to teach Tae Kwon Do in the United States, beginning his legendary career more than 50 years ago. A 10th-degree Black Belt, Grandmaster Rhee was trained directly by Choi Hong Hi, the South Korean army general who originally developed this modern martial art.

After coming to America in the 1950s, Grandmaster Rhee befriended Bruce Lee and introduced the celebrated martial artist to Tae Kwon Do. Since then, Rhee had also taught Muhammad Ali, Jack Anderson, George Allen, Sr., Bob Livingston, Tony Robbins, Jack Valenti, and more than 300 U.S. Senators and House Representatives. Today, hundreds of Tae Kwon Do studios in the U.S. and around the world use the Jhoon Rhee curriculum.

Around 1987-88 (three years later), I unfortunately had to move back home to Richmond, VA after learning that my father was having health complications.

I started working for a martial arts school in Henrico County at that time as the senior martial arts instructor. I was excited for this opportunity to continue my professional kickboxing journey and teaching martial arts because now I have this invaluable experience to share with students. After about seven years (1987 -1994) of teaching at that particular school, it grew to over 700 students at two locations.

When one door closes, another door opens and this next opportunity helped me to cultivate the teaching environment for Competitive Edge Karate.

There was a phone call for me at the karate school late one afternoon. It was a voice I had never heard before, from a gentleman who I had never met:

Hi, my name is Mark Glazier and I'm looking for top quality instructors to expand Master Glazier's Karate Studios in the New York, New Jersey and Pennsylvania areas and your name came up. I'm a former instructor and Black Belt under Jhoon Rhee and Jeff Smith.

Well after about a 30-minute conversation, I was saying to myself, "What just happened?" I had agreed to fly to New Jersey the next week and see this MGK operation he was describing. Once I arrived at the Newark airport, my designated driver picked me up and after our official greeting, he told me we have to wait for three other instructors. My first thought was, so I'm not that important and this call was made to several other instructors. I was ready to turn around, get on the plane and head back home.

This was a two-part interview. Part one was an interview with Mr. Glazier and part two was a tour of his MGK facilities, with his current instructors. It started with watching a lower belt level graduation at one of the schools. The school was designed like a fitness center, not a karate school. The graduation itself was normal but the energy level was very impressive for a lower belt level graduation. After the ceremony, we had a chance to have a private conversation with the instructors and get a better feel for the organization. It was interesting because I had fought professionally against two of the instructors, so that was a good icebreaker. The night ended with all the visiting instructors giving their opinions about the graduation. That was an awkward position to be in, but it was good to hear what the other instructors thought.

We spent the next day observing how they taught classes at two of the schools. Then each guest instructor had to teach 20 minutes of class, whatever they wanted to teach. Mr. Glazier had a private conversation with us that night at dinner and made his final decision and then we left the next morning. He made it clear that he didn't pull any punches and didn't have time for any BS. I was the only instructor he asked to come back and he thanked us all for our time.

Master Glazier's Karate International Inc. was the first publicly traded martial arts company on NASDAQ. I had to learn the curriculum and all the operational procedures within a month. These weren't easy tasks considering the quick turn around time; stress of moving my family and tying up loose ends, but made even more challenging with my Dyslexia. There were a lot of learning curves but I didn't want to screw up my opportunity. This level of teaching and operating schools was high pressure and physically demanding. MGK was also in every martial arts magazine at the time, so a lot of eyes were on us.

I spent three years working within that environment and again without a doubt there are no words to describe the experience I gained. Except let's just say, **"Nothing Beat Experience"** and now I have it from one of the best operators in the business at that time.

The Process

Martial Arts schools are known for helping children gain more confidence and become better focused; therefore, they became the go-to place for children who were diagnosed with Attention Deficit Disorder (ADD) and Attention Deficit Hyperactivity Disorder (ADHD) problems. I spent two years working with a child psychologist who was also a Black Belt in the martial arts to learn more about ADD and ADHD. I developed successful methods on how to teach children with ADD and ADHD through this experience.

Then, another opportunity presented itself for me to add to my arsenal of successfully working with children with different capabilities. One day while teaching a new student their first class, I was faced with a kid who had an Intellectual Disability or ID. I had never worked with mentally challenged children before, but today was that day. So, with another obstacle and another challenge facing me, I went into "let's learn about it" mode again to identify the problem and work to overcome it.

Throughout the last twenty-four years, I've had more than 100 students with learning spectrum challenges who have reached the level of Black Belt.

Continuing my learning on how to become a more effective teacher, there was another "ah-ha" moment. The life skills that I had learned through my personal adversities were starting to show up in my teaching. It became a clear and compelling fact that children need to learn these lessons of failures and achievements to understand how important it is to make good choices and really think about becoming independent.

My Early Life Lesson

One of the life lessons I had to learn at a young age and I like to share it because it is applicable for achieving goals – it was my responsibility to train hard to win a championship; not my trainers, sparring partners, friends or parents, but mine. That was a tough lesson because it felt like nobody cared. It's easy to get lost in thinking only about the challenges and obstacles before you. Instead, think only about your ultimate destination.

"I don't focus on what I'm up against. I focus on my goals and I try to ignore the rest."

~Venus Williams

A Martial Arts Statistical Fact:

In martial arts today, if one hundred people begin participating in a form of martial arts classes half of them will drop out within the first month (50 left). After six months of training half of them will drop out (25 left) and half of that group will drop out within a year (12 left). Out of the 12 remaining students, half of them will go on to achieve their Black Belt (6 left). At best, three will remain training after Black Belt (3 left) and out of those three students; two will quit before 2nd degree.

Humbly and Respectfully, My Successes Continued at CEK

Under my tutelage at Competitive Edge Karate, I have produced over 450 martial arts Black Belts with 11 State and National Kickboxing Titles and 1 World Amateur Kickboxing Title.

I've had Competitive Edge Karate Black Belt graduates accepted into International Baccalaureate (IB) Programs at their schools, Gifted Programs in both middle and high schools and The Governor's School.

My students have also earned athletic scholarships, and many are attending some of our country's most prestigious colleges and universities.

A Message from the Master:

We all know that parents cannot always be there for their little loved ones. So, let us help them develop the tools needed for independence - not dependence.

Being purposeful in our teaching and parenting will give children a better chance of growing up with self-confidence in their own ability to take care of themselves.

THE EDGE FOR LIFE PRINCIPLES

We operate on a basic set of fundamental facts about life, and we believe these facts can be applied to all people, across time and place. For children to live happy lives and become independent, successful adults, they need to learn these certainties. But memorizing a principle does not mean that a person has learned anything.

At CEK, we teach these principles by demonstrating them consistently in our classes. Our goal is to help our student's figure these truths out for themselves—and embrace them for their own lives.

HOW PRINCIPLES APPLIED AT CEK BUILD RESILIENCE IN CHILDREN AND TEENS

Children who want to learn martial arts give us the opportunity to teach them life skills while helping them achieve their dreams. We fuel their motivation by giving them the opportunity to succeed—and to learn from mistakes. Giving students the chance to make choices encourages them to take responsibility and exercise self-discipline. Mastering the various levels of karate is demanding, requiring time and effort. But the reward is worth it, and the student knows that. By setting a plan and following through, our students learn how to earn success.

In the following sections, you will find a brief background about each principle, followed by a short description of how we encourage students to discover and implement them in their practice of karate and their lives.

The Competitive Edge Karate - Edge For Life program presents six principles that can help a person to achieve a life of happiness and success. Used in conjunction with the discipline and focus of martial arts training, the program can help the student / person to become more adept at facing the challenges of life, and at enjoying themselves in the process. By understanding and applying these principles, the student can improve skills which will be the equivalent of earning a Black Belt in Life.

EDGE FOR LIFE -TABLE OF CONTENTS

The Six Principles we help them to discover are:

1. THE FUNDAMENTAL YET UNIVERSAL LAW

2. THE PATH TO HITTING THE MARK

3. HOW TO UNCOVER THE POWER OF INDEPENDENCE

4. HOW TO DISCOVER THE ONE-TWO PUNCH STRATEGY

5. THE FRAMEWORK FOR SELF-ESTEEM

6. DISCOVERING THE GREATEST REWARD

- WHAT'S THE COMPETITIVE EDGE KARATE DIFFERENCE?
- REFLECTIONS OF ACTUAL CONVERSATIONS WITH CEK PARENTS

There are thousands of stories and examples of decisions made by parents that could affect the overall growth of their children. As parents we all make the same mistakes of protecting our children from mistakes, pain and disappointments in life.

These are six examples of long-term versus short term thinking from loving parents. It's not about right or wrong or good or bad it's about parenting. No magic books or magic wands to help us on this long and rewarding journey.

Acknowledgments

To all of the martial arts students, parents, coaches, teachers, child psychologists and early childhood educators who I've had the opportunity to teach and work with over the last 40 years, thanks for sharing your ideas and parenting lessons with me.

Chapter 1

THE FUNDAMENTAL YET UNIVERSAL LAW

"The more risks you allow your children to take, the better they learn to look after themselves."

~ Roald Dahl

One of the most universal lessons we need our children to learn is that the world operates under certain laws—and the laws apply to them just as they do to everyone else. The most fundamental of these is that their choices have consequences. Once they understand their choices impact their lives, they have motivation to focus on making good decisions and develop responsibility. As children grow up, their choices become more complex, and the consequences can be life changing. Teens often face choices about drinking and driving, smoking and drugs, relationships and sex. Those who have fully grasped that all their choices have consequences are more likely to choose wisely.

Experience nudges children to make the connection that their actions result in effects. The little girl, who ignores mom's advice, running out of the house without her coat, discovers that being cold is no fun. The novice soccer player who spends extra hours practicing dribbling, passing, and shooting improves his skills and is thrilled when he gets more playing time. The child who gets the chance to explore his ability to make things happen, within a safe setting, learns his first important lessons about the real world. He learns that some of his actions will lead to positive outcomes and some will lead to painful ones. He realizes he can think ahead and act for the outcome he desires.

At CEK, we strive to give students plenty of opportunity to practice making choices in a controlled, protected environment. To learn physical self-defense, we have them practice falling correctly, on mats, so they won't get hurt if they ever fall on concrete. When it comes to making choices, we let them experience reality on a small scale, including the experience of consequences, being both rewarding and painful. We want them to learn the lessons of cause and effect now, while we can keep the lessons safe and the pain minimal. Later, when we can no longer protect them, such lessons can be life shattering.

We encourage students to plan and take action, because mistakes lead to learning and the chance to improve. We look for opportunities to help them evaluate when they performed skills well and when they were off the mark, when they made good choices and when they didn't. This approach fosters an understanding of the benefits of sound judgment, honesty and self-responsibility.

Our instructors model risk taking and learning from their own choices. They will contrast good and bad decisions they have made, and discuss what they learned in the process. Our instructors help students practice this first principle by giving them choices, asking them why they made the decisions they made, what the outcomes were, how the student felt afterwards, what that feeling meant to them, and what they learned. Our purpose is to help them figure out: "I can learn from my choices and my mistakes."

Learning enhances achievement. We encourage self-motivation, effort, practice, and the development of self-confidence based on competence that has been demonstrated. At each belt level, students make choices that can lead to mastery of skills required for the next belt. This goal gives them a point of focus. Their choices and effort determine whether or not they will earn the belt.
You will see our instructors illustrate the benefits of life long learning and achievement by sharing their struggles and successes via personal stories or stories of people they know, including those they admire—as well as those they don't. They will encourage students whenever possible by identifying

advancements and improvements verbally and by honoring those who have mastered specific goals. The belt ceremonies are one example of such recognition. Our instructors want the student to learn: "My choices affect my life."

We want our students to develop a positive, practical approach to life. We want them to learn that the world is not their enemy—it is a place open for their discovery and success.

Reflections of Actual Conversations with CEK Parents

The names have been changed to protect identities.

Story One

Mom: Kyoshi, Grace wants to quit karate.

Kyoshi: Why? She is doing a great job in class.

Mom: She says it's getting too hard for her.

Kyoshi: Each belt level will become a little more challenging as you progress through the belt ranks. But remember that the students are also more focused and prepared for the next step.

Mom: But I don't want it to be too hard for her and take away the fun.

Kyoshi: Let's bring her in the office and talk about it. (Grace enters the office.) Grace, your mom has informed me that you want to stop coming to karate class. Is everything okay with your training?

Grace: It's just getting too hard and not as much fun anymore.

Kyoshi: What do we say in class about things getting harder to accomplish?

Grace: We keep trying and never give up. Some techniques are going to be a little harder to do.

Kyoshi: So, why would you want to quit?

Grace: The other belt levels were easy.

Mom: Kyoshi, should it be that hard? (Grace exits the room.)

Kyoshi: Mom, it's not that hard. Grace is finding out that she needs to pay more attention in class and I believe that's what she is referring to as hard.

Mom: Do you think giving her a month off would help?

Kyoshi: I don't think that would make it easier for her. But, what do you think we should do?

Mom: I want to give her a month off.

Kyoshi: I wouldn't recommend that from my experience of working with students but it's your choice.

Mom: Kyoshi, it's so tough with her.

Kyoshi: Being a parent is a tough but very rewarding job and kids are not going to always agree with us.

Life Lessons:

Everything that happens to us is a consequence of choices made. Often the choice we make is nothing more than how we react to a situation.

Chapter 2

THE PATH TO HITTING THE MARK

"You cannot make people learn. You can only provide the right conditions for learning to happen."

~ Vince Gowmon

As parents, we sometimes advise our children: "Pay attention!" During a baseball game, we encourage them to keep their eyes on the ball. "If you set your mind to it, you can do it," we reassure them when they face a tough challenge. In different ways, we are telling them to stay focused.

Why is this so important?

We have all seen what happens when people are not focused. Anything or anyone who comes along can distract them from their task. The young boy working on a classroom assignment gets sidelined by the conversation two other students are having behind him. He fails to complete the work and earns a poor grade. The little league player notices the butterflies and dandelions surrounding her in the outfield. She gets caught up watching them and misses the fly ball that comes directly to her—and her team loses the game when two runs are made on the play. When a person is not focused, they give up control of their mind. They follows any sensation that happens to occur, whether it is related to her goals or not. Consequently, the ability to achieve their goals is limited.

When a child stays focused, he maintains control of his mind, not allowing distractions to lead him astray. The little boy may "shush" his classmates or ask to move to a quieter spot in the room so he can complete his work and get a good grade. The little league player chatters to the batter as she waits for the pitch. When she hears the crack of the bat, she already has her eyes on the ball and her mitt open. The fly ball she catches is the last out of the inning, and her team wins by one run. When a person stays focused, they have taken the first step to achieving their goals.
Staying in control of your mind is a critical aspect of karate. During class, you will see and hear our instructors stress the importance of keeping focused. They will remind students who are easily distracted to keep up with the class and on task. They will give examples of how failing to maintain focus leads to missed opportunities and failure. When reminders and examples aren't enough, they will follow with consequences, making the connection between the choice to drift and its negative outcomes very clear. Their purpose is to help

the student understand the value of "I will stay focused."

Focusing the mind is a choice that requires effort. Staying focused is a skill. Practice helps make it a habit; a habit necessary for achievement.

Reflections of an Actual Conversation with CEK Parents

Story Two:

Mom: Kyoshi, Michael doesn't want to assist in class anymore because of what happened in class last week.

Kyoshi: Let him know everyone makes mistakes and it's ok.

Mom: He's really sad about it.

Kyoshi: That's a big part of learning Mrs. Jones. We're going to make mistakes but again it's okay and the students didn't realize that anything was wrong.

Mom: I think it would be best for him to take a small break from helping you in class.

Kyoshi: Mrs. Jones it's only once a week for 30 minutes and he's teaching something that he likes.

Mom: Kyoshi, do you think that's too much responsibility for a 12 year old.

Kyoshi: Remember mom that's what we're trying to teach him.

Mom: Can you apologize to class for him?

Kyoshi: Mrs. Jones the class doesn't know he made any mistakes, plus as a Jr. Black Belt in class the class actually looks up to him.

Mom: I just don't want him to feel bad.

Life Lessons:

Setting a goal, no matter how simple, is always the easy part.; everyone has goals. The real challenge is not determining if you want the result to reach the goal, but if you are willing to accept the sacrifices required to achieve your goals.

Chapter 3

HOW TO UNCOVER THE POWER OF INDEPENDENCE

"To raise a child who is comfortable enough to leave you means you've done your job. They are not ours to keep, but to teach how to soar on their own."

~ Anonymous

Parents and teachers have a paradoxical goal: to work themselves out of a job. We want our children and our students to become independent thinkers—not followers who allow others to think for them. Our approach helps students combat peer pressure, as well as the influence of the media and other external sources. We teach students that nothing can replace personal responsibility or independent judgment.

Independent children don't look to others to decide what they should do. They look within themselves. They are comfortable making their own decisions. They decide which sport, or which instrument, to play. They don't blame their choices on others, preferring to acknowledge, "I did it "rather than claiming," they made me do it." They take responsibility for their actions, good and bad, and they are comfortable acknowledging an achievement. They know when they have earned recognition.

Independent children don't look to others for approval. Because they believe in their own judgment, they are insulated from peer pressure. Socially, they may feel left out from time to time, but when they are confronted with choices about relationships, drug use, and lying or cheating, they think for themselves. At CEK, you will see instructors act as role models using independent thinking and introspection about their thinking. They will talk not only about their thinking, but also about how they evaluated their thinking. ("I asked myself: is this what I want to do? Instructors will give students the opportunity to practice by asking students what they think and why, giving them choices and asking why. Their goal is to help the student decide: "I will think for myself."

Reflections of an Actual Conversation with CEK Parents

Story Three:

Mom: Kyoshi, my son is afraid of sparring class.

Kyoshi: Most beginner students have lots of fears about sparring in class.

Mom: I don't want him to get hurt.

Kyoshi: Beginners are only learning how to block and avoid techniques in the classes. So, he would have time to build his confidence level up before any actually sparring.

Mom: Can he miss that part of class on Wednesdays?

Kyoshi: No, Mrs. Smith. I'll help him to overcome this one obstacle in class. Keep in mind that the students in class with him are also afraid of contact.

Mom: But I know him and if he gets hurt, he will quit.

Kyoshi: I understand that this is a tough part of training for some kids and parents, but with your support I can get him through this.

Mom: I don't know now if that's what I want for him.

Kyoshi: This will help with other hard challenges in life and this is really a safe challenge.

Mom: I think it might be better at this time to cross that road at another time.

Life Lessons:

To help a child reach his or her full potential, we first have to understand their inner drives. Then we must offer the best guidance and environment for them to strive. This is where the foundation of the personality can be formed.

Chapter 4

HOW TO DISCOVER THE ONE-TWO PUNCH STRATEGY

"When we give children advice or instant solutions, we deprive them of the experience that comes from wrestling with their own problems."

~ Adele Faber

If children are to become successful adults, they need to know how to set and achieve goals. Achievement requires thinking for the long term, and this is a lesson that children come to understand gradually, through practice. It may take a few experiences of blowing an entire allowance on junk before a child learns the value of saving up for something important. A student may have to learn the hard way that not practicing his katas at home results in failing the tests in class. If he wants to earn the belt, he has to plan ahead, making time for homework and karate practice, along with all his other activities. He may have to forego afternoons of television or video games.

To overcome the challenges and obstacles that might block their path to success, children need to develop qualities that will see them through tough times as well as good times. If they perform poorly in class or fail a belt test, they need to figure out why this happened and plan to resolve the issue by the next test. The same applies to poor performance in an academic subject or any other area of life. To bolster their resilience and perseverance, children need self-discipline and personal integrity.

We help our students on the road to success by teaching self-discipline, perseverance, and willingness to delay gratification. By encouraging students to focus on the big picture and develop strategies for setting and achieving goals, we help them to discover that they have the patience, determination, persistence, and self-motivation to succeed.

You will see our instructors demonstrate long term thinking by sharing their early dreams and what they had to do, as well as the choices they had to make, to achieve them. Our instructors will help students practice long range planning and effort by asking them about their dreams and encouraging them to state their goals clearly. They will help students develop plans to achieve their goals, celebrating small and large victories along the way. Each belt is a celebrated achievement. They will also support students who experience setbacks, providing encouragement and guidance for improving. Their goal is to help the student choose: "I will plan and act for the long term."

Reflections of an Actual Conversation with CEK Parents

Story Four:

Dad: Kyoshi, my son wants to take a break from karate classes.

Kyoshi: Why, he's starting to show more confidence in class.

Dad: I know and that's a great thing.

Kyoshi: Okay Mr. Johnson, now I'm a little confused.

Dad: We signed him up for karate classes to build his confidence. But now that I see more confidence in him, I think it's time to try baseball again.

Kyoshi: That's great, but if you take him out of karate classes I don't think you're going to see the same confidence level.

Dad: I'll bring him back after baseball season is over.

Kyoshi: Mr. Johnson, when you first brought your son to his first introductory class here at Competitive Edge Karate he cried.

Dad: Yeah, I remember.

Kyoshi: This has been a six month process to get him to demonstrate that level of confidence in class. If you take him out of this environment, do you think that progress is going to continue?

Dad: I would hope so.

Kyoshi: Sir, a volunteer baseball coach isn't going to be concerned with your child's confidence level. It's little league baseball and if you're not a natural at hitting and catching the ball then it's back to the bench. What happens then, Sir?

Dad: I didn't think about that.

Life Lessons:

If you want to live a life filled with success — you need to be long-term oriented and stop falling for the short-term instant fulfilments. Live in alignment with your ambition, goals and dreams — and act in a way that actually improves your future.

Chapter 5

THE FRAMEWORK FOR SELF-ESTEEM

"If children feel safe, they can take risks, ask questions, make mistakes, learn to trust, share their feelings, and grow."

~ Alfie Kohn

As much as we might wish or try, we can't make our children respect themselves or believe in their own worth. Self-esteem is a combination of self-confidence and self-respect—both of which must be earned. To be seen as worthy of esteem, a person requires evidence of competence, evidence that one has value to oneself, based on personal actions. That's why we call it SELF-Esteem.

When a young girl works hard on a term paper and gets an "A", she adds that information to her tally of what she can do well, and why she can call herself a good student. She gains self-confidence and self-respect. If she didn't write the paper she turned in, she knows she isn't worthy of the "A" she received. She can't honestly call herself a good student, and she knows that any pride she pretends to feel is false. She didn't earn the grade by her actions, and her recognition of that fact diminishes her self-esteem.

The reward of receiving a belt also adds to a student's self-esteem—if the reward is earned. A student who meets all the requirements and passes all the tests deserves to get the belt. Students know that they have earned their right to be proud, as well.

But a student who is "given" a belt even though they have not met all the requirements or passed all the tests knows that the evidence shows them to be undeserving. They are robbed of the right to be truly proud and the belt does not hold the same meaning or value compared to the belts earned by students who passed all the tests. They are also robbed of the opportunity to develop the skills needed to overcome obstacles later in life—persistence, renewed effort, self-evaluation and commitment. If they recognize the discrepancy between their performance and what they were given despite that performance, they are robbed of self-esteem and the tools they will need to develop it in the future.

A second outcome in these situations could be even more damaging for long term success and happiness. A child who is given a belt even though said child did not pass the tests may choose to ignore the facts of the performance and decide that they deserve the belt, despite those facts and the requirements for earning the belt. They may want the belt so much that they will deny the reality it was not earned to others—and to themselves. The teacher who awards an unearned belt helps such a student take their first step away from accepting personal responsibility for the actions, away from honesty, and away from integrity.

Learning to make good choices, to act long term towards worthy goals, to think on your own—these all feed into the development of self-esteem. We seize every opportunity to help our students acquire the skills and build the character they will need to face life's challenges with personal strength and a sense of pride in who they are.

You can observe our instructors promote the importance of earning self-esteem when they ask students to evaluate themselves and their feelings of competence and worthiness after accomplishing specific achievements. They reinforce each student's independent evaluation of the rewards ("How did getting the belt make you feel? Why?"), the justice of the reward ("Did you think you deserved it? Why?"), and its meaningfulness ("What does having the belt mean to you? What does this say about you, to you?"). Our goal is for each student to learn: "I am proud of myself because I earned it."

Reflections of an Actual Conversation with CEK Parents

Story Five:

Mom and Dad: Kyoshi, would you have a few minutes after class to talk?

Kyoshi: Absolutely

(Parents in the office after class)

Kyoshi: What's on your mind?

Mom and Dad: Kyoshi, after much consideration and watching your program; which we love. We think that your standards for the kids are too high.

Kyoshi: Well thanks and why do you say that?

Mom: A lot of students are failing their belt level test the first time around.

Kyoshi: Yes m'am, and that's a big concern for you I see.

Dad: Well Kyoshi, we think that maybe you could consider some small changes that would help the students out.

Kyoshi: And that might be – What?

Mom and Dad: We're not sure right now but thought we would bring it to your attention.

Kyoshi: Let me ask you guys a question, are there any other parents with this concern?

Mom: I'm not sure.

Kyoshi: Okay, would you like for me to make it easier for all students to pass?

Dad: Not easier but maybe a break on the first testing.

Kyoshi: Mom and Dad, what are your goals for Stuart?
Mom: (with a very quick answer) To be a RESPECTFUL AND SUCCESSFUL kid.

Kyoshi: Do you think the world is going to give him a break?

Dad: I sure hope so.

Mom: He's a great kid.

Life Lessons:

Self-esteem is important because it heavily influences people's choices and decisions. People with high self-esteem are motivated and persistently strive towards the fulfillment of personal goals and aspirations. Self-esteem refers to a person's beliefs about their own worth and value.

Chapter 6

DISCOVERING THE GREATEST REWARD

"The work of education is divided between the teacher and the environment."

~ Maria Montessori

Happiness is a consequence of successful action. Happiness is the over-arching emotional reward an individual experiences when living life to the fullest, when pursuing worthwhile goals—both material and spiritual—and achieving them. This is what we want for our children. We want them to grow up and be happy, to achieve full, purposeful, and joyful lives.

People who pursue long-term happiness make their choices with a sense of personal responsibility towards their own lives. We see the earliest flickers of this orientation in the very small child who wants to dress herself or make her own bed. We see it in her desire for friends to share her interests and values, because friendship brings her joy. A teen pursuing long term happiness will make decisions about the activities she will participate in, the boys she will date and the parties she will attend based on whether or not they are good for her. People who are committed to pursuing happy lives realize that they must take care of themselves.

As parents, some of the most difficult and critical lessons we can teach our children are to value themselves, to think for themselves, and to choose and commit themselves to achieving goals that will enhance their lives.

At CEK, we want our students to develop a healthy sense of self and self-responsibility. By emphasizing that a person should take care of himself, and why, we teach children that this is a valuable goal. Goal setting begins within this context. We then bring in the issue of integrity, acting consistently toward values, which are in his best interests. This requires our students to remember the lessons about choices and consequences, about planning and acting long term, and about thinking for themselves.

You will see instructors give examples of thinking and acting for their own happiness by telling stories of their decisions based on self-interest (I wanted to be, to do, to feel proud of myself, to prove to myself, etc.). They will model the life satisfaction they have experienced as a result of approaching their decisions from a long-term perspective. They will encourage students to think in this regard by asking why they are making certain choices, what outcomes they are expecting, and why those outcomes are important to them. Our purpose is to help our students choose: "I will act in my best interest." From there they can use the other five principles to make their goals—and their happiness—a reality.

Reflections of Actual Conversations with CEK Parents

Story Six:

Mom: Mark has really worked hard for his test Kyoshi. Do you think he will pass?

Kyoshi: He needs to get one more stripe before testing, which is in three days.

Mom: Kyoshi, the green belt has been a struggle for him and I don't want him to lose his confidence.

Kyoshi: I understand, but he has to get that last stripe requirement for testing. Mom, how much is he practicing at home?

Mom: I don't know for sure.

Kyoshi: Let's bring him in the office and see. (Mark enters room.) Mark, how much are you practicing at home?

Mark: A lot

Kyoshi: Great, but you do understand that you need to earn your last stripe before testing, right?

Mark: Yes Sir. I understand, but it's getting hard.

Kyoshi: Do you need some extra help?

Mark: Probably, I guess.

Kyoshi: Let's meet for 15 minutes before your next class. (Mark leaves the room.)

Kyoshi: Mom, Mark has not been practicing at home and I think testing *next* month would give him more time to prepare and take off some of the pressure.

Mom: Can he just get the belt anyway? He has really been struggling to get the last stripe for testing.

Kyoshi: Do you want me to give him the stripe even though he hasn't earned it?

Mom: Yes, I think it would help.

Life Lessons:

Our job as parents is to guide and encourage positive learning from different experiences. Provide your child with the skills needed to rebound from setbacks and pave the way to success, so they can enjoy life.

Food For Thought:

Most would agree that overprotective parenting is probably not good for children.

Most would also agree that it is and yet, the trend toward so-called "helicopter or snowplow parenting" grows stronger each year. On the surface, this type of parenting might seem like parents are paving the way for their kids to succeed.

But this style of parenting can actually prevent children from developing critical coping skills. If healthy and happy is the goal, there is such a thing as too much safety.

Parenting is stressful enough—think empathy and compassion, not criticism.

What Makes It Different – The Dabney's Method

Competitive Edge Karate is a specialty-training center that has a very unique method of training. CEK incorporates physical fitness with an emphasis on personal development and coaching life skills through the martial arts. This creates an atmosphere and environment that thrives on giving your best effort.

The CEK System approach to training has as its core basic Self-Defense training and includes two critical methods of instruction:

1. The Master Instructor Method: The Master Instructor demonstrates, shares knowledge and wisdom while correcting students' mistakes. Strategies in this method include providing comprehensible feedback, modeling the correct technique and asking students to first reflect on their own work.

2. The Coaching Method provides support for student learning through motivation and encouragement. In this method the coach is not a subject expert, but is focused on helping the student to unlock their own potential. The best coaches are positive, supportive, trusting, observant, respectful and goal-oriented.

In the CEK System, both teaching styles are important to allow all students to reach their full potential.

The CEK structure includes five essential system components to be physically and mentally successful:

1. Personal and Emotional Development
2. Physical Fitness
3. Academic Achievement
4. Self-Defense Awareness
5. Unshakeable Confidence

The CEK System offers the dynamic movements of Tae Kwon Do, the discipline and power of Karate, the mindset of a Champion and is supported by over forty-years of martial arts experience!

Mastery is defined as having comprehensive knowledge or skill in a subject.

This unique martial arts training system is ONLY offered at CEK. IT IS NOT JUST ANOTHER KARATE PROGRAM! The framework of the CEK training system, belt level curriculum development, and physical training procedures are packaged in a unique manner. The CEK System is supported by research and delivered to its students based on documentation of 40+ years of tested and proven success!

Because of Kyoshi Roger Dabney's path of training and personal achievements, CEK students can learn martial arts within a system of study that offers a vast amount of experience through the eyes of a coach/instructor and champion. This kind of experience is rare within today's martial arts industry.

Some Achievements from the Master:

· Amateur Featherweight Kickboxing Champion
· Professional Welterweight Kickboxing Champion
· Member of the USA 3-Man Karate Team
· Ranked World Top Ten Kickboxing Champions
· Hall Of Fame Inductee
· Promoted over 450 Black Belt Students
· Head Coach of 11 National Kickboxing Champions
· Head Trainer for Lightweight Amateur Kickboxing World Champion
· Professor (Kyoshi Title) American Open Style Karate
· Master Instructor in Tae Kwon Do

A good coach can change a game. A great coach can change a life.

-John Wooden

At Competitive Edge Karate, our Purpose is to help you get the Edge for Life.

At CEK, we teach you how to recognize dangerous situations and how to defend yourself. That includes being able to neutralize your attacker when necessary.

However, our purpose is much larger. Life is about more than surviving to fight another day. It is about living well: being successful at the kind of life you want, being proud of your accomplishments and of your character, living up to your potential, and living with joy and happiness.

To get the Edge for Life, you will need to develop yourself in three areas: Physically, Mentally, and Spiritually. These are critical components to living independently, successfully, and happily.

The Physical Edge: Confidence in Your Body

Your body is your means to accomplish all action in your life—so take care of it!

Physical fitness is a basic requirement. Our program helps you develop Strength, Flexibility and Endurance, so your body can work for you, not hold you back. Strength gives you the power to rise to physical challenges. Flexibility lets you stretch beyond your previous limits. Endurance keeps you from wearing out before a task is done. When your body is fit, you feel healthier, and you can perform better physically and mentally—no matter what challenges you may face.

Training your body in self-defense is your means to protect yourself and others from harm. At CEK, we teach skills from several martial arts practices to give you a well-rounded, versatile arsenal of options when you are in danger. Tae kwon do, karate, jiu-jitsu and kali are all included in our multi-range system that helps you adapt to any threatening situation.

The Mental Edge: Confidence in Your Mind

Your mind is your means to decide what actions to take—so use it well!

The first step in using your mind is learning to stay focused. Without focus, a person is easily distracted. He misses important information and he forgets his goals. When you focus your mind, you are able to recognize danger as well as opportunity. Staying focused is a mental practice stressed throughout every CEK class, from the opening meditation to the closing ceremony.

Good judgment requires accepting consequences, good or bad. Part of making decisions includes assessing options for action. In a dangerous situation, you need to assess the level of threat. You need to be able to figure out if you can avoid an attack. That way, nobody gets hurt. If attacked, you need to decide how to respond. Do you strike—and if so, how hard? For every decision, you must accept the consequences that follow.

The same is true for decisions you face every day. Is it more important to practice katas for class or play video games? What will the consequences be, if you are not prepared for the next belt test? What is likely to happen if you spend extra time studying for a test in a difficult subject—or put in extra hours on a tough project at work? What will happen if you put it off?

At CEK, our instructors encourage the development of good judgment by holding you accountable for your decisions. Through experiencing success and frustration in the dojo, you develop your mental skills for making better decisions in the outside world.

Good judgment requires independent thinking. You can make your own decisions—or you can let others make them for you. Whichever way you choose, you still have to live with the consequences. Should you do a combination wrong just because the students in your row are doing it that way? Or should you watch yourself in the mirror and do it the way the sensei showed you? What happens when you have to demonstrate that skill to the master? Will it help you pass the stripe test? Should you hang out with your friends even though they are doing something unsafe? What are the potential consequences? Do they really care about you if they ask you to do something that may bring you harm?

Instructors at CEK encourage independent thinking in the classroom by getting you to focus on your personal skill development. The Martial Arts are individual practices, including individual mental effort. They emphasize self-development and self-improvement. People may come and go from your life, but you always have to live with yourself and your decisions. When you keep this in mind, you maintain independent control of your mind.

Good judgment is necessary for success and happiness in the long term. In life, if you want to achieve certain goals, you have to know what is required for success. Then you need to commit to taking the correct actions and follow through. If you allow yourself to be distracted or frustrated, for any reason, you may not reach your goals. Success requires persistence and effort. The same is true in the CEK dojo. If you want to move to the next belt level, you have to know what is required. Then you must decide to master the correct combinations and movements and follow through. We help you develop the mental discipline necessary for maintaining your commitment and achieving your long term goals for success and happiness.

The Spiritual Edge: Confidence in Your Character

Your character is your means to self-esteem and happiness—so build it with integrity!

Your character is built through your actions, which are based on your thinking. What you think and decide determines what you do. What you do determines who you are in the eyes of the world and, more importantly, in the eyes of the person who looks back at you in the mirror. Your mind and body, your thoughts and actions must be coordinated if you want to achieve a specific positive purpose. This is true when the goal is becoming a Black Belt, and it remains true when the purpose is to become your best self, to achieve your highest potential.

When you keep working towards difficult goals, despite hardship, your character expands to include self-discipline. When facing future challenges, you know that you have the ability to persevere.

When you achieve a difficult but worthwhile goal through commitment and effort, your self-confidence grows. You learn that you are capable of taking your potential to higher levels—in the dojo and in the outside world. Knowing that you can achieve your goals is the first step in developing self-esteem.

When you take pride in your accomplishments, you form the basis for self-respect. You recognize that you are worthy of these achievements. You earned them through your ability, your hard work, and your commitment. This type of pride is an inner knowledge. Knowing that you deserve to be proud of what you have done, of who you have become, is the second step to self-esteem.

Building your character with integrity means acting consistently to your goals and values. A person with integrity honors his commitments to himself as well as to others. Self-discipline, self-confidence, and self-respect become habits of character. They are habits that help you develop self-esteem and live happily. They are habits of excellence that give you the Edge for Life.

BEYOND KARATE CLASS

At Competitive Edge Karate, our goal here is to help parents and students transfer the lessons learned at CEK into every aspect of their lives—so our students will maintain their Edge For Life.

Online material, booklets and handouts will be provided for parents.

They will cover ways you can incorporate the principles we use in class into the way you interact with your child. They will include discussions and strategies for dealing with the challenges and the joys of parenting.

OUR MISSION

Competitive Edge Karate's mission is to create an environment that supports Personal Development with a Champion Mindset. Helping students to reach their Fitness Goals while developing an unshakable Confidence level to defend one's Self-Worth.

Personal Accomplishments

Roger Dabney, the Master Instructor of Competitive Edge Karate has been in the martial arts for more than 40 years. Kyoshi is a title that is bestowed upon an instructor of the martial arts. There is a ranking system for belts and levels of Black Belts and there is also a system of ranking for instructors. The title of Kyoshi is the equivalent to the term "Professor".

Career and Personal Achievements

- 2020 - Author of Book (Overcome Adversities While Discovering Life Skills) Through Martial Arts Training
- 2018 - Joe Lewis Eternal Warrior Award
- 2017 - Inducted in the Action Martial Arts Magazine and Hall Of Honors
- 2016 - Inducted in the AMAA Who's Who Legends in the Martial Arts
- 2016 - Master Glazier Karate Lifetime Achievement Award
- 2015 - Inducted in the U.S.A. Martial Arts Hall Of Fame; Recipient of the Living Legend Award
- 2012 - 6th Degree Black Belt Tae Kwon Do under Grandmaster Michael Coles of Coles Martial Arts Academy
- 2011 - 8th Degree Black Belt American Karate Academies under founder Grandmaster Jerry Piddington

- 2011 - 8th Degree Black Belt American Open Style Karate under Grandmaster Danny W. Wilson
- 2001-2010 Head Coach with 11 National and 1 World Kickboxing Titles
- 2003 - The Living Legends Sports Award, presented by Hanshi Jerry Piddington, Jeff Smith, Bob Wall, Don The Dragon Wilson, Joe Lewis and Howard Jackson
- 2000 – Developed *Fit for Life* Kickboxing Video.
- 2000 – Owner of Patent on *T-Power Target Pad.*
- 1999 – 5th Degree Black Belt Tae Kwon Do under Michael Coles and Joseph Drabkin, products of Jhoon Rhee Institute.
- 1996 – 4th Degree Black Belt under Master Mark Glazier – Founder of Master Glazier Karate in NY, NJ, PA.
- 1994 – Top Contender for Professional United States Welterweight Title. Lost to #1 Ranked Fighter in the World from Yugoslavia.
- 1994 – 10th Ranked Kick Boxer under PKC sanctions.
- 1994 – Won Professional Virginia Welterweight Title from 3-time State Champion.
- 1992 – 5th Degree under Dan Wilson, American Open Style Karate System.

- 1991 – 5th Degree under Legendary World Heavyweight Kickboxing Champion Joe Lewis.
- 1986 – Participated on the United States Karate Team under Jeff Smith.
- 1983 – Fought first Professional Kickboxing Match.
- 1981 – Won Amateur VA State Title in Kickboxing, age 17.
- 1981 – 1st Degree Black Belt under Dan Wilson, American Open Style Karate

"It's not enough to have lived. We should be determined to live for something."

—Winston S. Churchill

Samurai Warrior

Made in the USA
Middletown, DE
23 May 2023

30753310R00046